"Klint reminds us that reading scripture in the most powerful way means to be invited into a conversation. In daring and moving ways, he invites believers and non-believers to listen deeply and respond authentically. Klint provides an excellent way to prepare our hearts for the season, and for life."

Randy Harris
Author/Theologian

"Klint's voice is one I've come to trust. In this must-read collection of Advent meditations, he invites us deeper into the story of scripture; and as we read, we are allowed to bring our questions, our failures, our tears, and our fears. The devotional pieces are creative, honest, and ultimately hopeful – since they point to the One who came in flesh and blood."

Mike Cope
Pepperdine University/Author

"Advent is such a special season on the Christian calendar. What if we were to enter into dialogue with others about it – from prophets and apostles to the curious and doubters? Ask about their personal experience of Him? Interact with them through our own experiences? Invite our non-Christian friends to overhear the conversations? Klint Pleasant invites us to do just that. Readers will be blessed and enriched by this book!"

Rubel Shelly
Author

"I've always known that Coach Pleasant was an impactful coach and leader, but he shows us here that he's also an incredibly gifted writer and thinker. Perhaps one of the reasons he's a successful leader is because he understands the importance of nurturing the whole person. Allow these devotionals to bless your life, and nurture your soul, as they have mine."

Jon Horst
General Manager, Milwaukee Bucks, NBA

"At a time when most people need inspiration, my former basketball coach Klint Pleasant gives us an outstanding tool and a faith-filled message centered around Advent. This is a must read!"

Jonathan Merritt
Pastor, Straight Gate International Church, Detroit, MI

LETTERS OF ADVENT

25
DAYS OF
MOVING FROM
LAMENT TO JOY

KLINT PLEASANT

Copyright © 2021 by Klint Pleasant.

All rights reserved. No part of this publication may be reproduced, distributed, or transmitted in any form or by any means, including photocopying, recording, or other electronic or mechanical methods, without the prior written permission of the publisher, except in the case of brief quotations embodied in critical reviews and certain other noncommercial uses permitted by copyright law. For permission requests, write to the publisher at the address below.

Fedd Books
P.O. Box 341973
Austin, TX 78734

www.thefeddagency.com

Published in association with The Fedd Agency, Inc., a literary agency.

Unless otherwise noted, all Scripture quotations are taken from THE HOLY BIBLE, NEW INTERNATIONAL VERSION®, NIV® Copyright © 1973, 1978, 1984, 2011 by Biblica, Inc.® Used by permission. All rights reserved worldwide.

Scripture quotations marked HCSB are taken from the Holman Christian Standard Bible®, Copyright © 1999, 2000, 2002, 2003, 2009 by Holman Bible Publishers. Used by permission. Holman Christian Standard Bible®, Holman CSB®, and HCSB® are federally registered trademarks of Holman Bible Publishers.

ISBN: 978-1-949784-88-6
eISBN: 978-1-949784-89-3

Library of Congress Control Number: 2021918638
Printed in the United States of America
First Edition

Dear Abbey and Julia,

In a world full of uncertainty, here's what I'm certain of: your mother and I passionately love you and always will.

PS You will definitely be on the "nice" list.

Love,
Dad

CONTENTS

Introduction 9

1. Dear Paul 11
2. PS Dear Paul 15
3. Dear Zechariah 19
4. Dear Peter 23
5. PS Dear Peter 27
6. Dear CEO of Macy's 31
7. Dear Mary 35
8. Dear Joseph 39
9. Dear Isaiah 43
10. PS Dear Isaiah 47
11. Dear Granny 51
12. Dear Asaph 55
13. Dear Psalmist 59
14. Dear David the Warrior 63
15. Dear David the Broken 67
16. Dear Job 71
17. Dear Doubter 75
18. Dear Habakkuk 79
19. Dear John the Baptist 81
20. Dear Hosea 85

21. Dear Mark 89
22. Dear Mark the Scrooge 93
23. Dear Matthew 97
24. Dear Struggler 101
25. Dear God 105

Epilogue Dear Santa 109
Final Letter of Encouragement from the Author 111

INTRODUCTION

I've always been drawn to letters. In a world where undivided attention, listening, and holding space is increasingly difficult to find, I'm all for bringing back the lost art of letter writing. Text messages are convenient, social media pings work fine, chatting on the phone is timeless, and, of course, old fashion face-to-face conversations are hard to beat. But a letter can't be interrupted.

A letter invites the reader to sit with the information—to process the words, reread and look back for understanding, be fully present with the message, and perhaps even look inward. There's no talking over others, no formulation of a response while someone else is talking, no walking away, no voices raised—the reader just sits with the message and lets it be what it will be. To me, that seems refreshing. Maybe an old-fashioned letter can still be the anecdote for connection and communication. In this busy season, I wanted to slow down and sit with it all—my questions, laments, and joys—and maybe find a little rest this Advent season. So, I wrote letters.

There's just one small problem with the letters on the following pages: we won't get a response. I'm confident that all these letters will be marked "Return to Sender." So why write them? Perhaps in the process of writing, asking, wondering, pleading, yelling, lamenting, crying, and laughing—something will happen to us. Maybe that very process will help us breathe a little easier; gain some inner strength for each day; and feel heard in a world that makes it tough to feel heard.

You've probably felt the sting of well-meaning words from the person who says they can relate because they have gone through "something similar." You likely also know those comments do not help. But most of us have also felt the power of simply being able to process uninterrupted, without anyone else telling us what to do or how to feel. We've probably experienced the feeling of simply being able to let it all out, knowing someone else will simply be a safe and quiet listener. That act between two people, when it happens correctly, becomes holy ground.

Truthfully, the answers aren't what help. The listener processes what they hear through their own experience, context, and bias. Even on a good day, any answer given still falls short of perfect and on a bad day, they can be downright destructive. So, this Advent season, we will invite God to listen. We'll invite John the Baptist, Paul, Mary, Isaiah, the Psalmist, and many others. We'll fire some questions at them, maybe even second guess them. And dare I say, share our perspective. But we will also, with deep humility, admit our love and total dependence on God from whom all knowledge and wisdom comes.

Elie Wiesel said, "people are united by questions. It is the answers that divide them."[1] So, this is a book of questions, sprinkled with reminders of hope. If we spent our time answering, surely this book would turn-off many people right off the bat. My hope is that my questions and struggles become your questions and struggles. The converse is true in my life: your questions and struggles have certainly become mine. This is what motivated me to write.

Let's struggle together. Ask together. Hope together. In that process, my prayer is that we will leave feeling more united. And we will do that in the form of letters. These letters will surely be "returned to sender," but in the process of writing, we believe something will happen. We believe these letters will add muscle to our faith and send us on our way a little lighter and a little more hopeful. These are my letters, and they are now your letters too. You have honored me by reading them.

---

1 Wiesel, Elie. "The Loneliness of Moses." Essay. In *Loneliness*, edited by Leroy S. Rouner. Notre Dame, Ind: University of Notre Dame Press, 1998.

DAY 1

DEAR PAUL

How can we thank God enough for you in return for all the joy we have in the presence of our God because of you? Night and day we pray most earnestly that we may see you again and supply what is lacking in your faith. **Now may our God and Father himself and our Lord Jesus clear the way for us to come to you. May the Lord make your love increase and overflow for each other and for everyone else, just as ours does for you. May he strengthen your hearts** so that you will be blameless and holy in the presence of our God and Father when our Lord Jesus comes with all his holy ones.

1 Thessalonians 3:9–13 (emphasis mine)

Dear Paul,

There is so much conviction in your prayer to the Christ-followers in Thessalonica. I've wanted to ask you for a while now, did you ever actually meet Jesus? Some scholars speculate that you grew up in Jerusalem, so the likelihood of you crossing paths with the Messiah might have been high. I know you had a conversion experience that was described as super-natural, but there are religious leaders today who claim similar experiences.

Did you spend any time with Jesus? Did you have long conversations with Him? Ask questions? Get answers? Were you an eyewitness to any miracles, teachings, or His crucifixion? Did you know Him? If you did, then I understand the conviction in your prayer. I mean, you asked Jesus to "clear the way" and to "make people's love increase." You even asked Him to "strengthen . . . . hearts." You seem convinced that Jesus works and moves with power in people's lives. You used strong words: "clear" and "make" and "strengthen." If you knew Him personally, I get it. It's easier to believe when you have personal experience, I guess.

I must be honest: my prayers do not possess this same conviction. In fact, I often wonder if I'd be a believer had I not grown up in a household of believers. Did I say household? I came from a family tree full of believers. But I like the way you came up, Paul. You had the full conversion experience. You were lost and then found, and once Jesus crept into your heart, you were never the same. Maybe the faith displayed in one's prayer life is directly related to the awesomeness of the conversion? I don't know. But, again, I want to know, did you actually know Him? And if so, what was it about Him that made you pray like this, believe like this, talk like this, write like this, preach like this, stay faithful like this?

I find it hard to pray this way. I find it difficult to believe like you believe. I know this: I have not met Him. I have not seen Him, witnessed a miracle, touched His hands, or heard His voice. But I don't think I want to. When Yahweh showed up in ancient times, people were scared to death and asked Him to never do that again.

But you know, Paul—I like Christmastime. And your prayer shows up from time to time as a suggested Advent passage. I feel closer to Jesus at Christmastime. I feel less scared at Christmastime. My faith seems to increase around Christmastime. I like that the angels announced to the shepherds, "Fear not." And Paul, this is my take on that: When God showed up in times of old, it was usually bad news. It was usually scary. But, when He decided to wrap Himself in skin, the pronouncement from the angel was "Fear not." I like that. Now He's a God that I can touch. Now He's a God I can talk to. Now He's a God I can interact with. Now He's a God I can ask questions. Now He's a God I can yell at and laugh with. I like that. Did you do these things with Him? If so, does that explain the conviction in your prayer?

I like Christmastime because God presented as a baby, and one can't be afraid of a baby. I collect nativity sets, Paul. I wonder why? Perhaps it's because I like the idea of God coming near—very near—and it not being scary. My prayers seem to be more authentic during Christmastime. I wonder if it's because He seems more accessible. Perhaps the closest I ever get to seeing Him, touching Him, and hearing from Him is during the season of Advent.

Christmastime is not just the season of anticipation or the moment of incarnation. For me, it's a reminder not to be scared. It reminds me that He came very near to us. It reminds me that He wanted to experience the world just as I did. It reminds me that He is approachable. It reminds me that He is, well, real. So, Christmastime puts a little muscle in my faith and my prayer life. If I knew Him, maybe I would always pray like this. But I do not. In a few weeks my prayers will go back to being trite, vanilla, and wooden. But during this Advent season—the only season when I feel dangerously close to Him—my prayer life will match yours, Paul.

Mary was in pain, baby Jesus was kicking, the star was shining, the shepherds were making their way, and Joseph was doing the best he could. Because of that reality, Lord, will you make clear the path, increase my love, and strengthen my heart today?

DAY 2

PS DEAR PAUL

"Do not be anxious about anything, but in every situation, by prayer and petition, with thanksgiving, present your requests to God. And the peace of God, which transcends all understanding, will guard your hearts and your minds in Christ Jesus."

— Philippians 4:6–7

Dear Paul,

This is my least favorite of your writings, Paul. I realize I'm in the minority on this one. Your words here have comforted millions and made others millionaires: Etsy artists, Christian authors and musicians, and even a few TV evangelists. But not me, Paul, not me.

"Do not be anxious." I wish hearing it from you was enough. But what seems to work for me is a stiff drink, a pill, or a long talk with a good friend to ease my mind of its confusion. That's what works for me, Paul; that's what takes the edge off. But your words alone? Not so much.

Well, there was that one time. I think it was around 3 a.m. The hallway floor at the hospital was cool and the paint on the walls was a dull green. I can't remember the nurse's face, but I remember her expression and what she said. She handed me some pearl earrings and said, "These were your wife's." One doesn't plan to be a widower at age twenty-nine.

The only time I think I had the "peace of God" you mentioned, I felt it. It lasted for a few minutes. It was like all the Bible verses I'd ever memorized, all the VBS homework that received gold stars, the thousands of hymns I'd sung, the countless Bible lessons and sermons, and even the smiles from the older Christians at a Sunday potluck joined into one cacophony in my mind and spirit and presented as peace. I felt the peace you speak of, and then it was gone—it hasn't returned since. Oddly enough, Paul, I wasn't praying. You say that peace such as this follows prayer, but that's not my experience.

I prefer some of your other writings. My favorites are:

- "When I am weak, then I am strong. Your power is made complete in weakness. Your grace is sufficient."
- "I know what it's like to be lonely."
- "I asked You three times to take the thorn away."
- "I'm frustrated, but not quitting. I'm perplexed, but hanging in there; I'm hurting, but not in despair."

But here, in your letter to the Philippians, you tell us not to be anxious. I can't agree. I'm anxious, Paul. But the Advent season—the manger scene, the bright shining star, the shepherds, the smell of the barn, the journey of the wisemen, Simeon getting to hold the Messiah before his last breath—they help take the edge off. No prayer, no request, no super-natural feeling helps—just the reminder that the Holy God came near and put Himself in the same position as me.

In Jesus's own way, while in the garden of Gethsemane, He sat in a version of a cold, dark hallway, and was scared. That reality is enough. It's enough to keep me going. It's enough to give me hope. It reminds me that Jesus is on my side and might take issue with your words too, Paul. It gives me one little shot of peace at the end of the calendar year. It's just enough to take the edge off and to remind me that the baby King makes possible the reality of hope. It's not your words that bring peace. It's not your words that make me any less anxious. It's Advent. And because of Advent, that hope and that peace you speak of is just over the horizon.

DAY 3

DEAR ZECHARIAH

"Praise be to the Lord, the God of Israel,
because he has come to his people and redeemed them.
He has raised up a horn of salvation for us
in the house of his servant David
(as he said through his holy prophets of long ago),
salvation from our enemies
and from the hand of all who hate us—
to show mercy to our ancestors
and to remember his holy covenant,
the oath he swore to our father Abraham:
to rescue us from the hand of our enemies,
and to enable us to serve him without fear
in holiness and righteousness before him all our days.
And you, my child, will be called a prophet of the Most High;
for you will go on before the Lord to prepare the way for him,
to give his people the knowledge of salvation
through the forgiveness of their sins."

—Luke 1:68–77

Dear Zechariah,

I would have questioned the angel, too. If an angel approaches me and tells me something I believe is impossible, I'll have some follow-up questions. It just seems natural. Okay, okay, I hear you, but I do have a few questions.

Bam, you can't speak. Your tongue now weighs one hundred pounds. You've been shut up. I hear you, Zechariah. It doesn't seem fair. What does one say after months of divinely orchestrated heavy tongue disease? In my mind's eye, you can't get the words out quick enough or loud enough, "Praise be to the Lord!" Luke unmuted you with his pens and it was: "Praise be to the Lord!" That's what I would say, too, if I were convinced I had a conversation with God's messenger. But I haven't.

So, I stay on volume ten. I keep flapping my jaws. I have lots to say, but my message is very different from yours. My message is one of skepticism and questioning. I probably only believe because I was born a Christian. I heard prayers and hymns while in the womb. I was born on third base, as it relates to spiritual blessings and currency. I'm leery of people who talk like you, Zechariah. I want proof.

I tend to think people are willful. I believe people frequently are wired to manipulate the world to get what they want and then call it "blessed." So, I turn up my volume and say the opposite. Sometimes I feel like I was placed here on earth to encourage people to be intellectually fair and honest. I am useful when it comes to showing others that God's absence is what makes us stronger and more faithful. So, what the angel of the Lord ought to do during Advent is give me divine heavy tongue disease. I ought to swap places with you, Zechariah. Advent is a time to say, "Praise be to the Lord." Because God decided to wrap Himself in skin and come near. More than that, He even allowed a forerunner to shout that message with a megaphone, announcing His coming. Our modern-day response ought to be clear, simple, and loud: "Joy to the world, the Lord has come!"

PS You teach us a great lesson in parenting. It is not all about our kids. You were proud of Johnny, no doubt. You made that clear in the end of your poem. But ultimately this is, everything is, about Jesus.

DAY 4

DEAR PETER

Then the disciple whom Jesus loved said to Peter, "It is the Lord!" As soon as Simon Peter heard him say, "It is the Lord," he wrapped his outer garment around him (for he had taken it off) and jumped into the water. The other disciples followed in the boat, towing the net full of fish, for they were not far from shore, about a hundred yards. When they landed, they saw a fire of burning coals there with fish on it, and some bread. Jesus said to them, "Bring some of the fish you have just caught." So Simon Peter climbed back into the boat and dragged the net ashore. It was full of large fish, 153, but even with so many the net was not torn. Jesus said to them, "Come and have breakfast."

JOHN 21:7–12

Dear Peter,

I love reading about you in the Gospel of John. I can relate to you. Even though Jesus was your best friend and you knew Him personally, you were still fully human and made big mistakes. Reading about you messing up actually gives me hope and causes me to think Jesus can love someone like me because I know He loved you.

I'm reminded of the last nine chapters in John's Gospel, and in those last chapters, we only hear from you a few times. Oddly enough, your emotions and actions were all over the place. In chapter 13, you told Jesus that you would die for Him. He began to tell you and your friends that His death was just around the corner, and you interrupted Him to make it clear that anyone coming for Him had to go through you first. You told Him you would lay down your life for Him. But after that encounter, we don't hear from you for a while.

You showed up again in chapter 18, and your attitude and heart had changed. We now hear you denying the existence of Jesus. You told people you didn't even know Him. Wow. That's quite the change. You turned your back not just on the Savior of the world, but on your best friend. And as we read on in John's Gospel, we, again, don't hear from you for a few more chapters.

I'm sure you were off to yourself somewhere, contemplating your colossal failure. I think I would've been. But an interesting thing happened in the twenty-first chapter of John's Gospel. You reappeared. I was thinking that if you reappeared, you'd be begging for forgiveness or asking the disciples to pray for you and with you or mourning the loss of your best friend. But that's not what happened. Instead, you decided to go fishing. How interesting. And you asked the disciples to join you. How ironic. There you were, back in the boat, doing the same thing you were doing when Jesus called you out of that lifestyle a few years ago. It seems that you'd washed your hands of Jesus and restarted your old fishing business.

I've become convinced that at this point in the gospel story, you believed you'd failed Jesus and there was no hope for you. I don't blame you for feeling that way. And with that reality, you might as well go back to your old life; get back to what you know best. You stunk at being a Christ-follower, but you were certainly a good fisherman. But then Jesus showed up on the shore, and you did something that brings tears to my eyes each time I read it. When you noticed that it was, in fact, Jesus on the shore, you jumped out of the boat and swam to Him.

You came face-to-face with Jesus on the shore of Tiberius. You were out of breath, soaking wet, covered in sand, and locking eyeballs with your best friend. The last two times you were in His presence, you told Him you'd die for Him and then you said you didn't even know Him. This was quite the encounter. I think the entire gospel hinges on this moment between the two of you. Of all the things that could have been said, how was the tension and silence broken? Jesus invited you to breakfast.

He cooked a meal for you and called you to sit down at His table and eat with Him. At that moment, I'm convinced you breathed a sigh of relief, for in that moment, He'd forgiven you. In a few hours you'd tell Him you love Him three times over, but it's this moment when you realized He still loved you and had forgiven you.

I always like to revisit this story around Christmastime. Because the Christmas season ushers in a time when we enjoy a meal with family and friends: some of them we haven't seen in a while, and some of them, perhaps we would rather not see. It's one of the few times a year I actually sit around a table, Peter. Around that table during Christmas, I'm reminded of this encounter. That reminds me that when I sit with others around food, Jesus is present; and when Jesus is present, it means forgiveness and grace and mercy and reconciliation are too.

Thanks, Peter. Thanks for making the Christmas season more meaningful. Because the meal you and Jesus shared with one another reminds me of the meals I will share with others. And because it's Christmas, those meals will include the presence of Christ, and the presence of Christ means there will be an abundance of love. Merry Christmas—let's eat.

DAY 5

PS DEAR PETER

But do not forget this one thing, dear friends: With the Lord a day is like a thousand years, and a thousand years are like a day. The Lord is not slow in keeping his promise, as some understand slowness. Instead he is patient with you, not wanting anyone to perish, but everyone to come to repentance. But the day of the Lord will come like a thief. The heavens will disappear with a roar; the elements will be destroyed by fire, and the earth and everything done in it will be laid bare. Since everything will be destroyed in this way, what kind of people ought you to be? You ought to live holy and godly lives as you look forward to the day of God and speed its coming. That day will bring about the destruction of the heavens by fire, and the elements will melt in the heat. But in keeping with his promise we are looking forward to a new heaven and a new earth, where righteousness dwells. So then, dear friends, since you are looking forward to this, make every effort to be found spotless, blameless and at peace with him. Bear in mind that our Lord's patience means salvation, just as our dear brother Paul also wrote you with the wisdom that God gave him.

— 2 Peter 3:8–15

Dear Peter,

Hypocrisy, as you know, is claiming to have a certain set of standards or beliefs while your behavior fails to live up to those standards. I tend to place hypocrisy into tiers and categories so I can give myself a free pass. After all, my flubs seem harmless. But you, the one who claimed to be an apostle and as, the author of this passage, your level of hypocrisy is on red alert.

Where do you want to begin? You were a liar. You were unfaithful. You were disloyal. You had a temper. You didn't listen well. You talked too much. Perhaps your biggest indictment of all is, when your friends needed you the most, you were a no show. Then you sat down to pen a letter to early Christians and had the audacity to tell others to "live holy and godly lives."

This is hard to read from a guy who didn't "walk the walk." When Jesus needed you the most, you ran. When Jesus needed you to stand up for Him, you threw Him under the bus and drove over Him a few times. When Jesus needed you to have a steady hand, you thrashed your sword around like a fool. And now, here you are, telling others how to live. It's just hard to read, Peter.

But it is the Christmas season, and if there is ever a season when I'll slow down and look inward, it's Christmas. It's just so hard to walk around for six weeks and see the innocent baby Jesus, knowing He would go to the cross, and not examine my own heart a bit. So, let me try to self-reflect. The truth is, I'm no different than you, Peter. I'm sorry for sounding so harsh earlier in my letter. If I'm being honest, my rap sheet is just as long, and just as filthy because there are so many things I wish I could take back, or worry what people would think if they knew, or actions I'm ashamed to say I took.

Maybe the difference is that you forgave yourself and could boldly claim to others to pursue holiness and godliness while I still live in shame, guilt, doubt, and fear. Or maybe I need to realize something else. It's Christmas, which always brings good news. You began your Advent passage by reminding us that the "Lord is patient, not wanting anyone to perish." Gosh, I love that line. I'll say it again, "The Lord is patient, and He does not want anyone to perish." I suppose that is true regardless of the severity of your sin or the length of your rap sheet.

Christmas is the event that transitions God from a vengeful and firm presence to an angelic baby. This transition is full of grace and mercy and patience. That reality came to fruition as the baby grew up to be Jesus. God, in the person of Jesus, was so incredibly patient with you, Peter. At one point we are even told that after Jesus was resurrected, one of the first things He said was, "Go tell the disciples, and Peter" (Mark 16:7).

That seems redundant because you were a disciple. Why did Jesus say, "and Peter?" Maybe it's because Jesus knew you needed the personal reminder that He loved you. Christmas is a reminder of this same truth: God shifted the way He shows His love and patience. Instead of holding back punishment from His people, He laid it all on His only Son, the One who came as a baby at Christmas. So, maybe Christmas is the advent of patience. Christmas is the advent of love. Christmas is the sort of event that makes it possible to love someone as filthy as you and all of us.

DAY 6

DEAR CEO OF MACY'S

After they had heard the king, they went on their way, and the star they had seen when it rose went ahead of them until it stopped over the place where the child was. When they saw the star, they were overjoyed. On coming to the house, they saw the child with his mother Mary, and they bowed down and worshiped him. Then they opened their treasures and presented him with gifts of gold, frankincense and myrrh.

— Matthew 2:9-11

Dear CEO of Macy's,

I realize you're in the retail business which means your goal is to make money—lots of money. But I'd like to ask you to consider stocking some nativity sets this year that match the biblical story. I'm quick to admit that most of your sets are beautiful. Each year, I struggle to decide which one to purchase because I like them all. It's such a difficult decision: the one made of wood, the one made of crystal, the one that lights up, the miniature one, or the one with real pieces of hay. Last year I bought the one that was made of pewter, and I love it.

However, more than anything, I would love for you to stock a nativity set that follows the story we read in Matthew's Gospel. Other than the aesthetic differences mentioned, each of your sets are pretty similar. All of them include Mary and Joseph, the shepherds and the wisemen, baby Jesus, and, of course, the angel and the shining star. You see, I like to read Advent Scriptures from the Bible each year, so I am pretty good with the details. I'd like to respectfully request that you try to stock at least one option that is biblically accurate. I'll explain.

The scene most of us know so well includes the holy family in the manger with the shepherds, the angel, and the star, and the funky wisemen are off to the side. But the biblical account of Jesus's birth only includes Mary, Joseph, baby Jesus, the shepherds, and the angel—and they were at an animal stable. But the wisemen and the guiding star were not there. The Gospel writer Matthew tells us that when the wisemen arrived, they came to the house. So, it seems that we need a second nativity set which would include a house and the wisemen with Mary and Joseph as well as a Jesus who is likely a toddler. Just think of all the money you'll make with this second option available to consumers.

Perhaps you're wondering why I care about this. The reason is that I like Joseph. He modeled how to be a good dad. He was worn out, exhausted, and nervous about the fact that he was the earthly father of the Savior of the world. It sounds like time for a vacation, a stiff drink, or at least paternity leave. But no, not for Joseph. He got to work and provided his little family with a house. He put a proper roof over his boy's head. His son would go on to live most of His life as homeless, but not on Josephs' watch—no, not then. Joseph's got his boy a house.

I recall a time in my life when I was worried because I was absolutely drained. I had nothing in my tank, nothing left to give or offer.

I was physically and emotionally spent due to years and years of navigating a difficult thing in my life. When I finally fell into my own father's arms, cried, and told him I wanted to cash it in, I will never forget what he said. He said, "Son, you are stronger than you even know. You have no idea what you're capable of. You are so tough and resilient. Trust me, as your father, I know you can do this." Do you know what? He was right. I found a way to keep grinding. That's what good fathers do—they keep grinding.

Mr. CEO of Macy's, I'll be looking for this new nativity set which includes the house. And I'm hoping Joseph is prominently displayed. Because Joseph reminds us that Christmas is our inspiration to keep going, even when our tank is empty.

DAY 7

DEAR MARY

And Mary said:

"My soul glorifies the Lord
and my spirit rejoices in God my Savior,
for he has been mindful
of the humble state of his servant.
From now on all generations will call me blessed,
for the Mighty One has done great things for me—
holy is his name.
His mercy extends to those who fear him,
from generation to generation.
He has performed mighty deeds with his arm;
he has scattered those who are proud in their inmost thoughts.
He has brought down rulers from their thrones
but has lifted up the humble.
He has filled the hungry with good things
but has sent the rich away empty.
He has helped his servant Israel,
remembering to be merciful
to Abraham and his descendants forever,
just as he promised our ancestors."

> Mary stayed with Elizabeth for about three months and then returned home.
>
> — Luke 1:46–56

Dear Mary,

Your song occasionally shows up as an Advent reading. It is the familiar "Song of Mary." But oddly enough, Advent scholars stop at verse 55, just as you hit your last note. Sadly, verse 56 hangs out there in a land of nothingness. Completely forgotten. All alone. It doesn't necessarily attach as a beginning statement to verse 57, so I'm taking it upon myself to amend the Advent passage to include verse 56. It reads: "You stayed with Elizabeth for about three months and then returned home." This seems full of importance, if you ask me, Mary. Two pregnant women met: one carried the prophet of all prophets, and the other child, well, He would be the Savior of the world. Yes, you and Elizabeth had lots to talk about. So, Luke gave us what I will refer to as "the lost baby shower." It's tucked away and so insignificant that the Advent scholars leave it off the reading. But I've re-inserted it for you, Mary.

Yes, a baby shower for two pregnant women, each having boys. They had much to discuss, plan for, and be excited about. A little moral support from one another was in order: "How's Joseph holding up?" "Is Zechariah putting on any sympathy weight?" "I assume Joseph already has a crib made—he's such a good carpenter!" "I just pray for a healthy child." "I hope they grow up to be close." On and on you and Liz probably conversed. Yes, that's what expectant mothers do at baby showers; it's just normal chit chat.

I have to believe you two felt like any other soon-to-be mothers. Regardless of heavenly words from angels or crazy dreams, at the end of the day, you were both with child and excited. You were both probably overjoyed, counting down the days to when you would meet your little bundles of joy and they would trade the inner womb for your loving arms. Yes, this was a baby shower.

So, verse 56 brings normalcy to this situation. It settles things down. It gives you two moms your moment to be like any other pregnant, soon-to-be moms. This three-month long baby shower perhaps protects you from not knowing what the future holds. Because if you knew that, maybe you wouldn't be able to bear it. Praise God for protecting us from the future. He knows there's no way we could handle it.

You see, these two babies were leaping for joy in the safety of each of your cocoons, but it wouldn't always be this way. Your child would die on a cross, ultimately by suffocation, a cruel and painful way to die. Before that He would be betrayed by one of His closest friends, spat upon, and publicly ridiculed—and there wouldn't be a thing you could do about it. Elizabeth's child would end up getting his head cut off while in prison. And as the sword came down, he would doubt his own prophetic ministry and question if Jesus was even the Messiah.

But you women couldn't bear that information then. No way. So, God gave you your three-month long baby shower, like all expectant moms should have. Thank you, Lord, for protecting us from the future. If I possessed previous insight that I would have to bury my two girls, the weight of that reality would be too much to bear. Thank you, Lord, for keeping us ignorant of the future. We don't know what the future holds and that's good news.

Oh, one more thing, Mary. Advent changes this a bit. It doesn't erase the hurt, but it makes hope possible. Because of Advent, you can at least know that regardless of the future, there is a possibility of hope. These tragedies would be sprinkled with hope for the entire world. So, because of baby Jesus, we can utter the words "Merry Christmas."

DAY 8

DEAR JOSEPH

This is how the birth of Jesus the Messiah came about: His mother Mary was pledged to be married to Joseph, but before they came together, she was found to be pregnant through the Holy Spirit. Because Joseph her husband was faithful to the law, and yet did not want to expose her to public disgrace, he had in mind to divorce her quietly. But after he had considered this, an angel of the Lord appeared to him in a dream and said, "Joseph son of David, do not be afraid to take Mary home as your wife, because what is conceived in her is from the Holy Spirit. She will give birth to a son, and you are to give him the name Jesus, because he will save his people from their sins." All this took place to fulfill what the Lord had said through the prophet: "The virgin will conceive and give birth to a son, and they will call him Immanuel" (which means "God with us"). When Joseph woke up, he did what the angel of the Lord had commanded him and took Mary home as his wife. But he did not consummate their marriage until she gave birth to a son. And he gave him the name Jesus.

— MATTHEW 1:18-25

Dear Joseph,

I grew up in a conservative protestant Christian denomination, so I was never able to fall in love with your wife, mother Mary, the same way my Catholic friends did. But now—out of the oppressive stranglehold of legalism—I've enjoyed getting to know her. I now love visiting Catholic churches and seeing her. She deserves the love, after all, she is the holy mother of God's only child. Heck, I even have my own statue of your wife on my back patio and have been known to play the Beatles song, "Let It Be," and meditate as I gaze into her eyes.

We need not worry about Mary getting her due recognition during the Christmas season. We don't have to worry about the wisemen being short changed either. We can purchase all sorts of trinkets to honor and commemorate their place in the story. The shepherds undoubtedly have their place in the new bestselling version of the nativity set each year too—as does the angel and even the shining star. I suppose one could argue that you are properly honored because your figure is there as well.

But I think it's time you get some special attention. You have become one of my heroes, Joseph. I just don't think I could have negotiated the situation the same way you did. If my girlfriend comes home, tells me she's pregnant, and promises she hasn't been sleeping around on me, I'm probably packing my bags. Hey, I might be dumb, but I'm not stupid. Oh, to have the internal security you had. Of course, we don't have all the back-story details, but I've occasionally allowed my imagination to run wild. Perhaps you had coffee with your closest friends and sought out their advice. Maybe you said, "What should I do, guys? I have every right to give her a certificate of divorce. I mean, will I ever be able to trust her again? Her story is just so outlandish." On and on you could have gone. I would have.

Another Joseph, whom we read about in the Old Testament, inspired me as I made tough decisions when I was younger. The old story tells us Joseph was a man of integrity. The captain of the Pharaoh's guard, Potiphar, even hired Joseph as his personal caretaker and gave Joseph authority over his home. Joseph did not want to betray that trust. As you might remember, apparently Potiphar's wife noticed Joseph because he was easy on the eyes. Despite being chased by this beautiful, naked, and willing woman, Joseph escaped.

But the New Testament Joseph, you, have become my hero because you chose not to run away but to run toward something challenging. You pushed your chips in with Mary. And in doing that, you pushed your chips in for Jesus. You became the earthy father of the heavenly Son. Wow. Yes, we definitely need to put you front and center this Christmas. You believed the crazy story and placed your trust in the holy mother, who was not yet the holy mother—she was just your girl.

You're more than a good man, you are also a resourceful man. After the miraculous birth in the stable, you found a way to get your little family settled into a house. That's what good men do. So, I'm all for putting you back into Christmas because, if we have you around, the world has a chance. You were the one who was willing to trust a potentially sketchy woman. You were willing to be secure in your faith. You, while being exhausted and worn out, mustered up the energy to get the King of Kings settled into a proper house. I love mother Mary, and I love my statue of her. But tonight, Joseph, you get the attention. Tonight, when I pour a glass of vino, unwind on my patio, and turn on some tunes, my gaze will be on you. Because you are the backbone of the Christmas story.

DAY 9

DEAR ISAIAH

In the last days
the mountain of the Lord's temple will be established
as the highest of the mountains;
it will be exalted above the hills,
and all nations will stream to it.
Many peoples will come and say,
"Come, let us go up to the mountain of the Lord,
to the temple of the God of Jacob.
He will teach us his ways,
so that we may walk in his paths."
The law will go out from Zion,
the word of the Lord from Jerusalem.
He will judge between the nations
and will settle disputes for many peoples.
They will beat their swords into plowshares
and their spears into pruning hooks.
Nation will not take up sword against nation,
nor will they train for war anymore.
Come, descendants of Jacob,
let us walk in the light of the Lord.

— Isaiah 2:1–5

Dear Isaiah,

We live and function within a society that teaches us to have a common enemy. After all, a common enemy often unites us. Sadly, the most unified we have seen our country recently was just after 9/11: we had a common enemy, and we were on the same page. This plays out in small practical ways too. As a college basketball coach, I see it consistently every year between October and March. Even if the team isn't gelling and clicking on all cylinders, come game day it's easy to unite because we face a common enemy.

When it is time to fight, we don't need a plowshare or a pruning hook, we need a good sword and spear. After all, we have heads to chop off. An enemy stands in front of us, so we puff out our chests like young King David and march into battle against our enemy, the giant. But it's not enough to defeat the enemy, we must humiliate him. Cut off his head, take it back to camp and create a shrine for people to see it. The enemy is not only dead; he is very dead. Yes, a common enemy motivates and unites groups, and teams, and societies, and allies. Bring on World War III! When the dust settles, that's just about what we need to experience unity.

But you, Isaiah, point to another way. You remind us that Advent gives us something much different. You point to a prophet who was to come. This one would speak a prophetic word that, if adhered to, would end all wars. He would not only speak it, but He would also live it. In fact, in His darkest hour—at a time when war seemed almost justified—He asked His closest friend to put his sword away. His friend had cut off an enemy's ear, but He "touched the man's ear and healed him" (Luke 22:51). So, King David came by way of cutting heads off, but the Son of David came by way of putting heads back together. King David needed a sword, but Isaiah prophesied that the Son of David would not need a sword—it's quite the dichotomy.

You remind us, even if just for a few weeks out of the year, that we don't need a common enemy. We don't need a common enemy because God wrapped Himself in flesh and became a common Savior. At least for a few weeks, we have no need to bear arms, we have no need to fight, we have no need to conquer and claim territory, and we have no need to hurt others. Your prophetic word, Isaiah, is that because a baby Savior was born, we can take our swords and beat them into plowshares, we can take our spears and beat them into pruning hooks. Advent, and the baby King, show us that we now have no reason to fight, because now we have a reason to live.

DAY 10

PS DEAR ISAIAH

Oh, that you would rend the heavens and come down,
that the mountains would tremble before you!
As when fire sets twigs ablaze
and causes water to boil,
come down to make your name known to your enemies
and cause the nations to quake before you!
For when you did awesome things that we did not expect,
you came down, and the mountains trembled before you.
Since ancient times no one has heard,
no ear has perceived,
no eye has seen any God besides you,
who acts on behalf of those who wait for him.
You come to the help of those who gladly do right,
who remember your ways.
But when we continued to sin against them,
you were angry.
How then can we be saved?
All of us have become like one who is unclean,
and all our righteous acts are like filthy rags;
we all shrivel up like a leaf,

> and like the wind our sins sweep us away.
> No one calls on your name
> or strives to lay hold of you;
> for you have hidden your face from us
> and have given us over to our sins.
> Yet you, Lord, are our Father.
> We are the clay, you are the potter;
> we are all the work of your hand.
> Do not be angry beyond measure, Lord;
> do not remember our sins forever.
> Oh, look on us, we pray,
> for we are all your people.
>
> — Isaiah 64:1-9 (go ahead and read the whole chapter)

Dear Isaiah,

It's as if you take your readers to the carnival, Isaiah. You know the old carnivals that would come to town and set up in the supermarket parking lot or the abandoned field just outside of the city limits? I loved those as a kid. I didn't grow up going to Disney or any of the national brand amusement parks, but I did frequent a carnival or two. I remember the rickety sounds and the smell from the elephant ear stand, but more than anything, I remember the whiplash from the rides from getting jerked in one direction and then jerked in the other.

Whiplash was fun in that context. Whiplash as an adult is not so fun—and that is exactly what you do to your readers as they wait for Christmas. You begin by telling us of the glory of the Lord. You remind us that His presence is what we want and what we need. God is our great Helper; there is no one like Him. He fights our enemies, and He continually helps us. Heck, even Mother Nature bows to Him.

But then comes the whiplash. And it isn't the fun, laughing kind we remember as from the carnival rides; it's the kind that hurts and stings because your body is older and frailer. You give us all the warm and fuzzy good news and remind us of how great and wonderful Yahweh God is, and then you jerk our necks and hearts with one simple word: "But." You transition us with one word, and suddenly, it's not the quaint memories of the jerking on the tilt-a-whirl with our first love; it's more akin to the serious whiplash of a car accident. The kind that does real damage. In one word, Isaiah, you ruined Christmas. "**But** we continued to sin against Him and now He's angry. How can we be saved?" Question mark. That is an actual question. I mean you put the punctuation mark right there in your section of the Bible. Isaiah, you made it clear in one jerking motion that we are screwed, and then you asked: "How can we get ourselves out of this?"

As if the original whiplash weren't enough, you made sure we are good and sore. This is one of those injuries that starts at the neck and then travels all the way down the spine. You went on to say that we're all unclean; no, it's worse than that really, we're filthy. We're shriveled up leaves and full of so much sin that even God is hiding His face from us. God, the One who created us, is now hiding His face from us. This is bad. We aren't laughing and smiling on the tilt-a-whirl anymore, we're now walking through the old, rickety, always-horrific house of mirrors. And our worst nightmare is coming true: we're lost, alone, and afraid, and there are no trusted carnival workers or parents in sight to rescue us.

Just as our utter hopelessness sinks in, you introduce another word: "Yet." That's right, yet: "**Yet** You, Lord, are our father. We are Yours. You will choose to love us." And now, Isaiah, you bring us back to the tilt-a-whirl. The good feeling of whiplash. But you do even more than that. You introduce a new way. A way that will create a smooth transition from God to us—one that will never be rickety or harsh. Your "Yet" paves the way for Christmas. You know God has a plan to never again bring whiplash on His people, even if it's their own doing. Then you introduce us to one more word to make "Christmas according to Isaiah" complete: "**Rend**." You dusted off an old word for us: "Oh, that you would rend the heavens and come down." In other words, "tear heaven apart, rip it in two, come out, come back, come down, and join us." Just like that, you prophesied about the greatest holiday on the calendar, which brought us the greatest man we will ever know.

Christmas according to Isaiah is now complete. You give us the gospel story in three words, and that story culminates in Christmas. The King of Kings is coming to us. The heavens have been torn apart and the incarnation is upon us.

But, yet, rend. Like three gifts under the tree
But, yet, rend. Always smooth, always gentle
But, yet, rend. Merry Christmas.

DAY 11

DEAR GRANNY

Dear friends, now we are children of God, and what we will be has not yet been made known. But we know that when Christ appears, we shall be like him, for we shall see him as he is.

— 1 John 3:2

Dear Granny,

I was fourteen years old. We arrived just minutes late. When we walked into your house in Flint, Michigan, your husband—my grandfather—had drawn his last breath only moments before. The house was still and quiet. Your son, my father, broke the silence when he said, "We can talk if we want."

You were strong and composed—you had plenty of time to say your goodbyes. And then, three strangers walked through the door carrying a long black bag with a zipper. I watched as they zipped up your husband's body and carried him out the door; carried him out of his own house, where you'd both lived for forty years. And that's when you lost it. You grabbed the bag and screamed, "Don't take my Johnny. Please don't take my Johnny!" My dad held you, and you finally let go of the bag and collapsed in my dad's arms. My uncle whispered, "It's just a body; his spirit is gone." But you wanted the body.

Bodies matter.

I remember sitting by myself in a hospital hallway at 3 a.m. and being told by a nurse that in a little while I would need to identify my wife's body on the operating room table. Growing up, I overheard people say, "It's the spirit that matters, not the body." But nevertheless, I wanted to see her, to touch her one more time, to kiss her face.

Bodies matter.

Jesus was already dead, but the women (Mary Magdalene, Mary the mother of James, and Salome) were on their way to the tomb anyway to prepare the body, to honor the body, to anoint His body.

Bodies matter.

I am captivated by the opening verses in 1 John 3: "We know that when He appears we shall be like Him, for we shall see Him as He is."

What does the future hold? What will the future look like? What will we look like in the future? Christians have asked these questions for thousands of years. We are fascinated with it. We're curious. We're concerned. Some are scared. Some are anxious. I don't have the answers to all the questions on this matter. But I think the author of 1 John gives us at least a sliver of insight in his words here: "we shall be like Him."

Christmas reminds us Jesus was God incarnate. He came in flesh. He bled. He experienced the fullness of what it meant to be human. He was God, but He was also God's perfect version of a human, and "we shall be like Him."

The post-resurrection accounts in the Gospels give us some important clues too. He was recognized as Jesus; He had a body. His body had scars. He could communicate with others. He had his full range of senses, and He could be touched and felt.

In one Gospel account, He walked with, sat with, and broke bread with two disciples. In another account, He asked a friend to touch His scars as proof. And He was recognized on the seashore cooking breakfast over a fire and sharing a meal with His friends. "We shall be like Him." And of course, the Christmas story paints the picture of Jesus as a baby, fully human. We can hold Him, we can wipe His tears, we can swaddle Him, and we can sing and rock Him to sleep.

Our problem is that we have been heavily influenced by a particular worldview which teaches that the body is bad and that the spirit is good; the body can be destroyed, but spirit lives on. But the New Testament message, including both Christmas and the resurrection, takes bodily life seriously. In fact, the author began this very epistle by writing, "we have seen with our eyes . . . . we have looked upon . . . . we have touched." And the Christmas story has "body" written all over it. We have the stable, the parents, the shepherds, the wisemen—all physical beings who make the story accessible.

A person without a body was unimaginable in the Jewish tradition. In fact, early paintings of the afterlife do not show us what we so often think about today. We don't see angelic figures or clouds. Rather we see human beings interacting with and holding one another with facial expressions that indicate pure joy.

The ultimate proof that bodies matter is that God used one to reveal Himself in the person of Jesus. The New Testament insists on it as does Christmas. Faith in Jesus means He really was born, He really lived, He really died, and He really was raised from the dead into an authentic bodily existence.

The gospel depends on this, and it is the story of Christmas: God became a Person with a body.

Granny, Advent reminds us that Jesus came as a baby. We can relate to that. We know what babies look like. But John reminds us that because of Christmas, we also know what we will look like in the future. We need not fear, thank God. We begin our life looking like Jesus, and thanks to Christmas, we will end our life looking like Him, too.

DAY 12

DEAR ASAPH

For the director of music. To the tune of "The Lilies of the Covenant." Of Asaph. A psalm.

> Hear us, Shepherd of Israel,
> you who lead Joseph like a flock.
> You who sit enthroned between the cherubim,
> shine forth before Ephraim, Benjamin and Manasseh.
> Awaken your might;
> come and save us.
> Restore us, O God;
> make your face shine on us,
> that we may be saved.
> How long, Lord God Almighty,
> will your anger smolder
> against the prayers of your people?
> You have fed them with the bread of tears;
> you have made them drink tears by the bowlful.
> You have made us an object of derision to our neighbors,
> and our enemies mock us.
> Restore us, God Almighty;
> make your face shine on us,
> that we may be saved.

> You transplanted a vine from Egypt;
> you drove out the nations and planted it.
> You cleared the ground for it,
> and it took root and filled the land.
> The mountains were covered with its shade,
> the mighty cedars with its branches.
> Its branches reached as far as the Sea,
> its shoots as far as the River.
> Why have you broken down its walls
> so that all who pass by pick its grapes?
> Boars from the forest ravage it,
> and insects from the fields feed on it.
> Return to us, God Almighty!
> Look down from heaven and see!
> Watch over this vine,
> the root your right hand has planted,
> the son you have raised up for yourself.
> Your vine is cut down, it is burned with fire;
> at your rebuke your people perish.
> Let your hand rest on the man at your right hand,
> the son of man you have raised up for yourself.
> Then we will not turn away from you;
> revive us, and we will call on your name.
> Restore us, Lord God Almighty;
> make your face shine on us,
> that we may be saved.
>
> — Psalm 80

Dear Asaph,

What a beautiful song you have created. If Casey Kasem had lived in the ancient world, your song would have surely spent weeks on the Top 40 charts.

It strikes me as interesting that you make specific mention of the tune of your song. I love songs that have good tunes. When I think back to songs I enjoyed in my youth, I most remember the catchy tunes. Even though I still don't know all the words, I recognize those tunes when they're played. As much as I like The Temptations, Pearl Jam, and the Beatles, I can't say I know all the words to their songs. But I can recognize the tunes: one strum of the guitar, one beat from the drum, or one pounding of the keys, and my face lights up. But if you hand me a microphone and ask me to sing at Thursday night karaoke, I'll flub it.

What a wonderful thing when an artist can give us both a beautiful tune and lyrics. It's one thing to get a good tune, but when it comes together with quality lyrics, we have an artistic masterpiece.

The older I get, the more I notice the words, not just the tune. So, as I flipped through your Advent Psalm, I paid special attention to your lyrics. I noticed that you gave us not one, but three references to God's face. You asked God to make His face "shine on us." Maybe you were a little out of touch with the real world? You must have known your audience. I'm thinking the listeners of your song have heard the stories of Yahweh from their moms and dads and grandfathers and grandmothers. You can't look at God's face. Come on, are you nuts? One look at God's face and you're toast. Just ask the poor guy in *Raiders of the Lost Ark* that took one quick peek at the presence of God. Everyone in the ancient world knows you can't look at God's face. Just in case you don't believe me, let's do some quick reminiscing through the Old Testament:

- "You cannot see my face. No one can see my face and live." (Exodus 33:20, author's paraphrase)
- "Anyone who comes near the Lord will die." (Numbers 17:13, author's paraphrase)
- "We will surely die, for we have seen God." (Judges 13:22, author's paraphrase)

- "You speak to us, Moses, because if we deal directly with God we will die." (Exodus 20:19, author's paraphrase)

I'm thinking people loved your song for its tune, but they knew your lyrics were a little off. Maybe that's why you are clear to mention the tune at the beginning. So much for a musical masterpiece, this one looks like it will only spend a few weeks on the charts because everyone knows a good tune can only take a song so far. In the end, people want substance too.

Wait a minute, your song is an Advent song. Psalm 80 is part of the Christmas story; it shows up from time to time on the Advent calendar. We need to remind ourselves of that; it's an important piece of information. This changes everything. On Christmas, all those verses about God's wrath get tossed into the sea. Because on Christmas, God made Himself accessible. He made Himself tolerable to look at. Tolerable? More like, adorable. He became a baby, and who doesn't like to look into a baby's face?

The miracle of Christmas is the moment when God makes His face and presence something we can grasp, relate to, and feel safe around. There's no more fear and trembling because God isn't angry anymore. He is no longer just our Lord; He is now our Savior. That means your song is now so much more than a good tune—because of Christmas, your tune is now gospel. And that's a song we can put on repeat; it'll never get old. Your song reminds us that Christmas is the moment when a great tune and great lyrics meet up for the rest of eternity. Because of Christmas we can now look into the face of God and sing, "Joy to the world, the Lord has come." And the song won't just have a catchy tune, the lyrics will be on point too.

Because of Christmas, we have much more than the Lord's coming, we now have a Savior too.

DAY 13

DEAR PSALMIST

You, Lord, showed favor to your land;
you restored the fortunes of Jacob.
You forgave the iniquity of your people
and covered all their sins. . . .
I will listen to what God the Lord says;
he promises peace to his people, his faithful servants—
but let them not turn to folly.
Surely his salvation is near those who fear him,
that his glory may dwell in our land.
Love and faithfulness meet together;
righteousness and peace kiss each other.
Faithfulness springs forth from the earth,
and righteousness looks down from heaven.
The Lord will indeed give what is good,
and our land will yield its harvest.
Righteousness goes before him
and prepares the way for his steps.

— Psalm 85

Dear Psalmist,

Tucked away in verse nine of your Psalm is a little reminder that brings back memories from my childhood. You wrote, "Surely his salvation is near those who fear him." I grew up associating God with fear. He was the big eye in the sky; His eyes saw everything. He even had special x-ray technology and could see behind closed doors. This fear of the Lord created quite the fear in me.

I remember hearing a gentleman retell a story over and over about how he caught two young men he was mentoring doing something they should not have been doing. He started to approach them and noticed they were peeking around the corner, watching for any adults who might come by. When he finally got to them and "caught" them in the act he said, "I saw you looking around the corner for adults, but what you really needed to be doing was looking up because God can see you."

I understood why he said that, but the story never made me love God more—it only produced more fear. It's hard for me to process the idea that you associate this fear of the Lord with salvation and glory. Like I said, as a child I feared Him too, but I can't say it produced a healthy way of life. I did my best to avoid pitfalls because I was scared of God. My relationship with Him was simply transactional; all business. I'd do my part, and then one day God would do His part.

While doing doctoral work, I took a deep dive into the study of leadership. The research is clear that transactional and authoritative leadership only goes so far. Maybe we need to give you a free pass because, after all, you did write this a long time ago. Now we have more research and information to draw from, but you didn't have access to the latest and greatest scholarly work on motivation, love, and impactful leadership.

But this is a Christmas Psalm; it works its way onto the Advent calendar from time to time. This means we need to give it a fair and honest hearing. We need to pause, consider, and connect dots. In other words, we need to do a little research. You might not be surprised to know I just flipped over to the Gospels and read the Christmas stories according to both Matthew and Luke. (That's where people look when they want to understand Christmas according to the Bible, right?) On three separate occasions while retelling the Christmas story, both Matthew and Luke wrote some variance of "Do not be afraid." I like the idea of Matthew and Luke's phrasing, "do not be afraid" rather than the Psalmist's "fear Him."

Christmas according to Jesus agrees with me. Because the new covenant Christmas story removes the notion of fear. It says, "Don't be afraid." When I'm afraid or scared, I feel unsettled and nervous. I'm not productive. I'm not intrinsically motivated. But when someone tells me from the beginning that I need not fear, I become relaxed and at ease. Your Christmas Psalm must be read and understood within the entire context of the Christmas story. There was a time when we needed a healthy fear, no doubt. But after a little more research, we have discovered that when God became a baby and joined humanity, He removed all fear.

I've done the research. Relax, we need not fear because it's Christmastime.

DAY 14

DEAR DAVID THE WARRIOR

David ran and stood over him. He took hold of the Philistine's sword and drew it from the sheath. After he killed him, he cut off his head with the sword. When the Philistines saw that their hero was dead, they turned and ran. Then the men of Israel and Judah surged forward with a shout and pursued the Philistines to the entrance of Gath and to the gates of Ekron. Their dead were strewn along the Shaaraim road to Gath and Ekron. When the Israelites returned from chasing the Philistines, they plundered their camp. David took the Philistine's head and brought it to Jerusalem; he put the Philistine's weapons in his own tent.

As Saul watched David going out to meet the Philistine, he said to Abner, commander of the army, "Abner, whose son is that young man?"

Abner replied, "As surely as you live, Your Majesty, I don't know."

The king said, "Find out whose son this young man is."

As soon as David returned from killing the Philistine, Abner took him and brought him before Saul, with David still holding the Philistine's head.

> "Whose son are you, young man?" Saul asked him.
> David said, "I am the son of your servant Jesse of Bethlehem."
>
> — 1 Samuel 17:51–58

Dear David the Warrior,

Congratulations on starring in perhaps the most popular story in the most popular book ever written. That's quite an accomplishment. It's hard to find anyone, anywhere who's not familiar with the story of you slaying the giant: David versus Goliath. That phrase has been used over and over to bring attention to the underdog. There's no telling how many coaches have used this story, out of context I might add, to motivate their teams to a potential victory. I'm happy to tell you that I've never used your story like that, and I even coach for a living. I think there's something else going on here, and I wanted to run it by you since you're the star of the story.

Many people assume the story ends as soon as the giant fell to the ground. For years, I too thought that was the ending. I spent half my life just reading the children's version of your tussle with the giant. Later in life, I became curious and kept reading. Well, I discovered an entirely new meaning. And it has nothing to do with slaying the giants in my own life if I would just call on the help of God. I think you've shown us so much more than that. If we keep reading your story, we see that after you hit the giant in the head with a stone, you finished the job. Some people believe you killed him with your stone and slingshot, but Scripture tells us that you ran over to the giant, pulled his sword from his holster, and cut off his head. My goodness. This is like a scene from a gruesome war movie. But the story doesn't end there either. We then learn that you grabbed the giant's head and carried it into town and put his weapons in your own tent. At that point, it was safe to say everyone knew not to mess with you or your God.

After all of that, this part of your story ends with King Saul summoning you, wanting to know who you are. You showed up at the King's doorstep-with the giant's head in your hand and you told the King you were the son of Jesse. Then you added a little detail that practically jumped off the page when I read it: you said your father was from Bethlehem. And David, I must tell you that sent chills down my spine. Because when I think of Bethlehem, I think of Jesus. When I think of Jesus, I think of Christmas.

Oh, here's one more important dot that I connected: Your name is, of course, David. You won fights by cutting off heads. That's why I addressed this letter to "David the Warrior." But Jesus came as the "Son of David," and He showed us a different way. Jesus healed and forgave, even His enemies. He healed the servant's ear even as He was being arrested. He prayed for the ones who crucified Him. He was beaten, mocked, and hung on a cross—a most humiliating death—and He prayed for them. He prayed for His enemies when He could have destroyed them. Then, He took it a step further: He died in their place.

I admire your story, David, I really do. And I admire the warrior in you. But it's exhausting to think about having to do that much fighting just to keep winning. Your story paved the way for the "Son of David" to come and show us another way. Christmas is the story of winning without having to do any fighting. Because of Christmas, there are no heads to cut off. We can put our swords away and rest peacefully in His gentle love and care.

DAY 15

DEAR DAVID THE BROKEN

The Lord sent Nathan to David. When he came to him, he said, "There were two men in a certain town, one rich and the other poor. The rich man had a very large number of sheep and cattle, but the poor man had nothing except one little ewe lamb he had bought. He raised it, and it grew up with him and his children. It shared his food, drank from his cup and even slept in his arms. It was like a daughter to him. "Now a traveler came to the rich man, but the rich man refrained from taking one of his own sheep or cattle to prepare a meal for the traveler who had come to him. Instead, he took the ewe lamb that belonged to the poor man and prepared it for the one who had come to him." David burned with anger against the man and said to Nathan, "As surely as the Lord lives, the man who did this must die! He must pay for that lamb four times over, because he did such a thing and had no pity." Then Nathan said to David, "You are the man! This is what the Lord, the God of Israel, says: 'I anointed you king over Israel, and I delivered you from the hand of Saul. I gave your master's house to you, and your master's wives into your arms.

I gave you all Israel and Judah. And if all this had been too little, I would have given you even more. Why did you despise the word of the Lord by doing what is evil in his eyes? You struck down Uriah the Hittite with the sword and took his wife to be your own. You killed him with the sword of the Ammonites. Now, therefore, the sword will never depart from your house, because you despised me and took the wife of Uriah the Hittite to be your own.'

"This is what the Lord says: 'Out of your own household I am going to bring calamity on you. Before your very eyes I will take your wives and give them to one who is close to you, and he will sleep with your wives in broad daylight. You did it in secret, but I will do this thing in broad daylight before all Israel.'" Then David said to Nathan, "I have sinned against the Lord." Nathan replied, "The Lord has taken away your sin. You are not going to die. But because by doing this you have shown utter contempt for the Lord, the son born to you will die."

— 2 Samuel 12:1-14

Dear David,

You got yourself in quite the mess. It was one thing to sleep with another man's wife, but then you had to kill the poor guy too. Come on! You took a man's wife to be your own, knowing full well that she was vulnerable because her husband was off fighting a war over which you were the Commander in Chief. Then the innocent man, who was off fighting, got moved to the front lines to be killed, just to cover up your own mistake.

Here, you don't sound like the "man after God's own heart" as you're often described. This story of yours has always troubled me. I can deal with the infidelity part—that unfortunately happens from time to time. What really bothers me is that you killed the innocent man. Thank goodness you had a good friend in your life who could talk some sense into you. What a blessing it must have been to have someone like Nathan in your life. He had the courage to confront you.

But this is where the story really makes me angry. Nathan confronted you, and then he pardoned you on behalf of God. It's not the pardon part that makes me angry, but the fact that God punished an innocent baby. Because of what you did, God took the life of the infant born from your relationship with Bathsheba. That makes no sense to me and seems completely unfair. In my estimation, the punishment does not fit the crime. What had the baby done?

This story always makes me angry with God and, therefore, angry with you. But during the Advent season this story is a little more bearable, a little easier to process. Because I'm reminded that the Christmas season indexes another innocent baby who was killed. Of course. He was able to grow up a bit, but we all know Jesus was born crucified.

What you did was wrong, David. And the fact that the innocent baby was killed seems unfair. But God always works to find a way to keep loving us. And He ultimately showed this love through the death of another innocent man—One who happened to be His own son. He created Christmas knowing that He would eventually allow His own Son to be crucified. Because of that, now your son will live, David. And your sin is forever wiped away. Merry Christmas.

DAY 16

DEAR JOB

He is not a mere mortal like me that I might answer him,
that we might confront each other in court.
If only there were someone to mediate between us,
someone to bring us together,
someone to remove God's rod from me,
so that his terror would frighten me no more.
Then I would speak up without fear of him,
but as it now stands with me, I cannot.

— Job 9:32-33

Dear Job,

I hear you. I want my day in court with God too. The Psalmist reminds us that it is okay to express frustration to God. I mean, if you don't care about someone, I suppose you would never even waste your breath on them in the first place. So, maybe we're flattering God when we're upset with Him. I guess that points to the inkling of faith we have left.

I have never liked what God did to you, Job. You were going about your business like an upstanding citizen and then zap, God decided to use you as a pawn in a chess game with Satan. I grew up hearing your story, but I am embarrassed to say that I was probably in college before I knew your story had more than two chapters. I was well versed in the opening lines of the story and, of course, the torture that ensued from Satan. But for some reason, for me the story ended with you in a pile of rubbish and telling off your wife after she asked you to curse God because of all He'd subjected you to. So, I always equated your story with integrity in suffering.

But when my faith became my own in my early adult years, I saw clearer what you were all about. I like you much more now than I liked the simple man of integrity I assumed you were in my youth. I like the quick-tempered Job who was not afraid to question God and even got angry with Him. You became a trusted companion because I connect very much with that emotion. I get mad enough at God when bad things happen to me even when I know He did not cause them, so I'd hate to see how I might treat Him if I actually knew He was the author of my hurt.

I found myself rooting for you as you ranted and raved at God in the book we call Job. I still remember the day I discovered the hidden verse that mentions your wanting a day in court with God. You wanted your attorney to cross examine Him. You wanted a mediator—an umpire to call when it's a ball, a strike, a safe, or an out. I played a little baseball in my day, and it was always reassuring when the umpire saw things the way I did. When making a nice stab from my shortstop position after a ball was hit hard up the middle, I would sling it to my first baseman in time and hear the umpire yell, "He's out." Or I'd be rounding third base and turning on the afterburners to slide into home and hearing the umpire yell, "He's safe." There is nothing like hearing the umpire side with you—the good guy—and see it the way you see it, calling it out for all to hear: "He's safe."

So, your desire for a ruling resonated with me. In my college days, I think I even typed out those verses and hung them on my wall. What authentic and inquisitive thinking Christian doesn't want their day in court with God or doesn't want to hear the umpire's call? I know I do.

But Job, the Advent season and Christmastime remind me of something. Even though you didn't get what you wanted in that exact moment, God did hear your cry for an umpire, for a fair hearing in court. He knew the time would come when we would get what we wanted and needed. And that cross-examining attorney, that umpire we want, came in the form of a baby in a manger. That baby now stands between you and the God who allowed Satan to torture you.

I'm sorry you had to suffer so much. But I'm so grateful you called out for a mediator to settle this score. God heard you. He wrapped Himself up in a baby and made everything alright. That baby grew into a man, and He died for us. In His final breath, He yelled out, "It is finished." And that cry defeated Satan. I wonder if you heard that cry, but to your ears it sounded like, "He's safe."

We finally got our umpire, Job. He was born in Bethlehem, He grew up in Nazareth, and His name is Jesus. Merry Christmas.

DAY 17

DEAR DOUBTER

> I had heard rumors about You,
> but now my eyes have seen You.
>
> — Job 42:5 HCSB

Dear Doubter,

If you sometimes doubt, rest assured you're in good company. Prophets of old doubted, apostles who followed Christ doubted, even Jesus's cousin doubted Him. If you struggle with doubt, it's probably a good sign. Questions are good because they produce a desire to pursue truth.

If I can't see for myself as an eyewitness or experience something firsthand, my doubt grows. I have to rely on hearsay or rumors, and I know most rumors aren't completely true. So, it's hard to stake my claim on a rumor. It's hard to make decisions about how I'll lead my life based on hearsay. It's hard to build my hope around secondhand story. But every once in a while, a rumor is true. Now, what if the rumor is about the Savior of the world?

One of the first places I turn for comfort when I'm struggling with doubt, which is quite often these days, is the book of Job. It helps me to know Job doubted and questioned God. It makes me feel like my doubting is okay. Job walked with God and knew God but still doubted, questioned, and struggled. After decades of reading and rereading Job's story, I recently noticed something new.

Near the end of the story, after God gave His thundering response, Job piped back up and had the nerve to get the last word in. All these years, and I never noticed, but it's there: After God's monologue, and Job's patient listening, Job cleared his throat and said one last thing. But Job closed out his story by saying, "God, I'd heard rumors about you but now my eyes have seen." Imagine that: Someone hearing rumors about God, and then getting the chance to tell Him to His face, "You know, I've heard rumors about You. But now I've had the chance to see You face-to-face."

I'm happy for Job. He was a pawn in a cruel game between God and Satan. He had to endure trauma and untold suffering because God wanted to go toe-to-toe with Satan, and they needed someone who'd serve as guinea pig. Because of that, I love the fact that Job got his clarity, he learned the truth regarding the rumor.

I want my clarity; I want the truth too. More specifically, I want to know the truth about the rumor my parents told me while growing up. The same one told to me by my Bible teacher, my mentors, and my favorite authors. They've been speaking of this rumor that God is real; that the story of His Son is real. This rumor has been the center of my life, and now I am passing on this rumor to my children. I hope it is true. Some rumors I desperately want to be false, but not this one. If it's not true, my life has been fraudulent.

Maybe that's precisely the reason I love Christmas. Maybe I love it because of the idea that, on Christmas, the rumor gets transferred into truth. At least that's what I want to believe. God came for all eyes to see, for all hands to touch, for all ears to hear directly from God. Christmas makes the rumor true. He has come. He is here.

I can't personally see Him. But the rumor feels a little more believable because the shepherds saw, the wisemen saw, and Matthew and Luke wrote about it. I still struggle. But every year when I get out the tree, string up the lights, play holiday music, and gaze into the eyes of my nativity set characters—the rumor feels true. Christmas gives me hope. To all the fellow doubters out there, Christmas makes this rumor which haunts us believable.

DAY 18

DEAR HABAKKUK

> Though the fig tree does not bud
> and there are no grapes on the vines,
> though the olive crop fails
> and the fields produce no food,
> though there are no sheep in the pen
> and no cattle in the stalls,
> yet I will rejoice in the Lord,
> I will be joyful in God my Savior.
>
> — HABAKKUK 3:17–18

Dear Habakkuk,

I'm so grateful that biblical scholars of old decided to put your book in the Bible. It has become one of my favorite books. For one, it's nice and short, and that makes it easy to tackle in one sitting. Sitting to read the Bible as a youngster and not even making it through one book always bummed me out. But your book was an easy finish in one sitting, so I felt as if I accomplished something.

My repayment to you was selecting a passage from your writing the first time I spoke publicly in a church service. I was so nervous. But my familiarity with you put me slightly at ease, and I got through it. Years later, when helping a small, struggling church without a preacher, I decided to tackle an entire series on the Minor Prophets. Again, you were my inspiration. When I think of you, I think of deep and profound faith, a trust in God which is unmatched.

For over twenty years, I've made my living as a basketball coach, and the ending words in your book of the Bible rival any inspirational speech a coach could give. Apparently, things were difficult in your world. You opened your book with things like: "For the earth will be filled with the knowledge of the glory of the Lord as the waters covers the sea" (2:14). Wow, the Lord's love is immeasurable. But you painted a dark picture at the end of the book: No food, no crops, no animals—nothing left to sustain you. Yet you determined to remain hopeful. You determined to stay faithful to your God. You determined to keep your trust in Him.

You have become my hero because you were the first person I discovered in the Bible who refused to place your trust in things that have no power, and chose to show your reliance on Almighty God instead. Thanks, Habakkuk, you've put muscle in my faith. I often can't relate to your level of faith and trust, but around Christmastime I can feel like we're kindred spirits. Because in our hopelessness, your God sent His Son—an occasion we now celebrate during Christmas. Even with no vacancy, no warm clothes, no proper shelter, and no midwife to help, your God showed up. He revealed Himself to us in our hopelessness. Now, I have hope. You got there on your own, Habakkuk, but I needed a baby King to get me there. But either way, we are both now hopeful. Because of what God did on Christmas, I can now say along with you: "Even if there is no food on the shelf, clothes in the closet, money in the bank, or friend to laugh with—because of Christmas, I will still trust in Him." Because of your influence, this Christmas will be merry.

DAY 19

DEAR JOHN THE BAPTIST

In those days John the Baptist came, preaching in the wilderness of Judea and saying, "Repent, for the kingdom of heaven has come near." This is he who was spoken of through the prophet Isaiah:

"A voice of one calling in the wilderness,
'Prepare the way for the Lord,
make straight paths for him.'"

John's clothes were made of camel's hair, and he had a leather belt around his waist. His food was locusts and wild honey. People went out to him from Jerusalem and all Judea and the whole region of the Jordan. Confessing their sins, they were baptized by him in the Jordan River.

But when he saw many of the Pharisees and Sadducees coming to where he was baptizing, he said to them: "You brood of vipers! Who warned you to flee from the coming wrath? Produce fruit in keeping with repentance. And do not think you can say to yourselves, 'We have Abraham as our father.' I tell you that out of these stones God can raise up children for Abraham. The ax is already at the root of the trees, and every tree that does not produce good fruit will be cut down and thrown into the fire.

"I baptize you with water for repentance. But after me comes one who is more powerful than I, whose sandals I am not worthy to carry. He will baptize you with the Holy Spirit and fire. His winnowing fork is in his hand, and he will clear his threshing floor, gathering his wheat into the barn and burning up the chaff with unquenchable fire."

— MATTHEW 3:1-12

Dear John the Baptist,

Next to Joseph and Mary, it's hard to imagine anyone who believed in the baby King more than you. I suppose the shepherds could give you a run for your money, but by this time in Matthew's narrative they were already off tending to their flocks. Maybe the wisemen? After all, they went home by an "alternate route" because they were so convinced the baby was the Christ. But we must not forget that they were astronomers, and they did, in fact, stop by King Herod's palace on the way to find the star. So, they remain a tad sketchy. Maybe Simeon could be mentioned in this group? You remember, the old lad who got to swaddle God in flesh before he took his last breath. Nah, for all we know that was just so some stuffy scholars could say that an old prophecy was fulfilled.

So that leaves you, John.

Of course, we need to make sure that you are not confused with the apostle John. The apostle John fell asleep while Jesus prayed. That John was nowhere in the narrative when Jesus needed him the most. But you were much more committed than that. The Bible tells us on a few occasions that Jesus's disciples turned their back on Him, and perhaps the apostle John is lumped in with this group. So, I will do my part to make sure people don't confuse the apostle John with you, especially during Advent.

You were committed—you were all in. While Jesus was growing in "wisdom and stature," you were out running His PR campaign. You spent your time telling the entire region surrounding the Jordan about Jesus the Messiah. Although, "telling" is an understatement. You were a walking commercial, conjuring up all the shock value one liners you could muster. Your language repertoire included things like: "This is the guy Isaiah spoke of!" "Make straight paths for Him!" "He can raise people up out of stones!"

I hope all the new Christians out there who haven't yet memorized all the names and who's who never confuse you with the apostle John. New Testament readers will meet the apostle John soon enough, but you are the first John they meet, according to Matthew. You were the one who prepared the way for the Messiah.

Oh, to have faith like you. Oh, to be committed like you. If Jesus would have married one day, you were definitely "Best Man" material.

But I do feel like Bible readers need a word of caution. Sometimes I feel like I need to tell people to stop reading Matthew's Gospel at the end of chapter 3. It ends with Jesus being baptized by you, His best man. God seemed happy. The world seemed right. Heaven opened like a budding flower in springtime. You became the world's greatest evangelist. People believed and were saved. Jesus's own baptism was the icing on the cake. Advent is perfect. The end.

But if people must (if some happen to be those curious, "I want the full story," inquisitive kind of Christians), then they can read on. But I warned them.

You see, Matthew tells us later that you questioned the validity of the Messiah. A few chapters more and we see that you sent a messenger to ask Jesus Christ if He really is the Christ (the Messiah). You asked, "Is He the Christ, or should we look for another?" What were you thinking?

Here is my response to you as I read this a few thousand years later: "Thank you, John the Baptist!" Thank you for being real. Thank you for asking a hard question. Hard question? Strike that. How about *the* question. After all, you were about to be executed. You were in prison. They wanted your head on a platter, and it soon would be. If anyone should have been spared, it was you. If anyone should have asked questions, it was you. And if anyone deserved answers, it was you.

Of course, the so called Messiah did respond to you. Jesus sent word to you that the blind received sight and the lame walked again. Even though His answer spoke of fulfilled prophecy—prophecy you would know—I wonder if you still felt like you died in vain.

But it's Advent, so there must be a silver lining. What Advent teaches us is that even in the special star's shining, lavish gifts from astronomers, and miraculous appearances from angels, we might still doubt and struggle and wonder. We might even be put to death for believing in the Messiah. Advent provides the space for all that. And your story helps with that, John.

Matthew tells us that after you were beheaded, your friends retrieved your body, gave you a proper burial, then they told Jesus. And guess what, John the Baptist? When Jesus heard the news, He left crowds of people and went off alone because He wanted to be by Himself. He mourned for you. Because Jesus truly is the Messiah and because He went to the cross, as hard as your death was and as lonely as you felt, Jesus has your back. Because of Advent, you won't stay buried.

DAY 20

DEAR HOSEA

When the Lord began to speak through Hosea, the Lord said to him, "Go, marry a promiscuous woman and have children with her, for like an adulterous wife this land is guilty of unfaithfulness to the Lord." . . . The Lord said to me, "Go, show your love to your wife again, though she is loved by another man and is an adulteress. Love her as the Lord loves the Israelites, though they turn to other gods and love the sacred raisin cakes."

So I bought her for fifteen shekels of silver and about a homer and a lethek of barley. Then I told her, "You are to live with me many days; you must not be a prostitute or be intimate with any man, and I will behave the same way toward you."

— Hosea 1:2; 3:1–3

Dear Hosea,

I'm sure Jesus is supposed to be my favorite character in the Bible, but if I'm being honest, you are. I fell in love with your story the first time I read it. You were going about your life, keeping to yourself, being a good person, and then suddenly, your life got turned upside down.

God decided to use you to perform a sociology experiment, and you were the main subject in the research.

As you well know, your wife was extremely promiscuous. That's putting it nicely, I suppose. She would sleep with any guy that was willing. Nothing grosses me out more. You should have bailed on her, Hosea. I'm sure you could have found a woman in town who would have been loyal to you; someone who would have been content with your love and only your love. But God stepped in and decided to use your story as a social experiment for all of Israel.

He told you to stay with your unfaithful wife. In fact, He took it a step further than that. He demanded that you find her—in the act with one of her several side partners—and pay to take her back as your wife. I don't know how you did it, Hosea. My heart breaks for you. What you had to do sounds like pure torture to me. If my girl wants to sleep around, if I'm not enough, or if her idea of a good time is to sleep with every man she can, then she can hit the road.

But you received a command from God Himself to take your wife back and keep loving her and stay faithful to her—even when you were given no love or mutual loyalty in return. Life is not fair. And yet, once I realized what was really going on in your story, I fell in love with it even more.

Come to find out, Yahweh God was using you as an object lesson for the entire region. God's people had been unfaithful to Him for generation upon generation, and He used you as a tangible lesson to demonstrate how that felt. As far as I can tell, you are the only person in Scripture other than Jesus who was able to feel, in a sense, what God felt.

But I know the fact that this story helps others understand how unfaithful they've been to God probably doesn't ease your pain. You still had to endure a horrible situation. I know it sounds insensitive to say I know how you feel, but I think I do have a small taste of it. Even though good things have come from your situation, it was still incredibly difficult. But the pain is eased a bit at Christmas.

At Christmas, when I see God as a baby, when I see the trusted holy mother and the loyal father Joseph, when I see the faithful shepherds and the devoted wisemen—it takes the edge off. I can cope a bit better. Because Christmas reminds me God sent His Son to do the ultimate feeling on His behalf, for all eternity. Jesus took on all the painful feelings and all the suffering. And now, because of that, God never has to pass those feelings on to anyone else. But I know you had to endure it, Hosea. And I want you to know that every Christmas, I'm not just grateful for all the faces around the manger, I'm grateful for you too.

DAY 21

DEAR MARK

Another time Jesus went into the synagogue, and a man with a shriveled hand was there. Some of them were looking for a reason to accuse Jesus, so they watched him closely to see if he would heal him on the Sabbath. Jesus said to the man with the shriveled hand, "Stand up in front of everyone." Then Jesus asked them, "Which is lawful on the Sabbath: to do good or to do evil, to save life or to kill?" But they remained silent. He looked around at them in anger and, deeply distressed at their stubborn hearts, said to the man, "Stretch out your hand." He stretched it out, and his hand was completely restored. Then the Pharisees went out and began to plot with the Herodians how they might kill Jesus.

— Mark 3:1–6

Dear Mark,

Your Gospel re-telling is quick and action packed. It's the shortest of all the gospel narratives. The healing you write about in the third chapter of your Gospel is no different. The story moves quickly.

There was no warm, heartfelt conversation between Jesus and the oppressed. Jesus had a mission here, and He wasted no time. You tell us that He said, "'Stand up in front of everyone.'"

That seems a tad insensitive. I mean, after all, this person probably felt shame. He was disfigured. This is much different than your friend John telling us of Jesus redirecting attention from the woman caught in adultery when He bent down to write in the sand, perhaps giving the woman a second of relief so others' eyes were no longer on her.

Maybe the point of this healing is not the healing. Jesus used an object lesson to make a point to the Pharisees. Jesus showed His full humanity here. You tell us He was angry. Maybe you were trying to tell us that this was not a story of compassion for a disabled person. Maybe, Mark, you want us to know this is a story about the humanity of Jesus. I like this passage because we see Jesus get a little feisty. There will be plenty of times for Jesus to show compassion, but this person with the withered hand simply caught the residual benefit of Jesus's standing up to bullies. Jesus, at times, asked people to be quiet and not speak of the healing He performed. He said it wasn't His time yet and, perhaps, was delaying the plot of His murder. But here, Mark, maybe you show us that He is not going to be quiet anymore. Jesus is now ready to accept His cross; this story now pivots our focus to Jesus being crucified. That reality is now in Jesus's near future.

Your Gospel seems to focus on shame in a unique way. Your entire Gospel shows the shame of Jesus in the rejection from His own people, the abandonment of His disciples, and His death on the cross. But you also show how He overcame it. So perhaps this story in your third chapter is a microcosm of Jesus. How shameful this innocent man must have felt at being told to stand in front of everyone. Jesus was quick and seemingly uncompassionate. But maybe you were trying to show us something else, Mark, and maybe this connects to Advent.

Jesus called this person into His own world, which is a world of shame. Mark, even though you didn't write about it, do you remember the birth story, the Christmas story? It was a story filled with shame. The King of Kings couldn't even have a proper birth. He was born in a barn with shepherds for company rather than a midwife. Perhaps this is the most compassionate miracle of all. Because this man that you wrote about in your third chapter briefly walked the Via Dolorosa (the way of suffering) with Jesus. From this moment on, the religious leaders constantly plot to kill Jesus.

This man with the disfigured hand marks the beginning of the end for Jesus's earthly ministry. In a way, he helped carry the cross. He took on shame. He had the opportunity to walk the same road Jesus walked. He became the object lesson that set the greatest event of all time in motion, Jesus's death. Christmas is about Jesus being born. But you remind us He was born crucified. It would be a shameful walk, and this man walked it with Jesus. Thanks for this reminder, Mark. Withered hands, pierced hands—kindred spirits. Merry Christmas.

DAY 22

DEAR MARK THE SCROOGE

The beginning of the good news about Jesus the Messiah, the Son of God, as it is written in Isaiah the prophet:

> "I will send my messenger ahead of you,
> who will prepare your way"—
> "a voice of one calling in the wilderness,
> 'Prepare the way for the Lord,
> make straight paths for him.'"

And so John the Baptist appeared in the wilderness, preaching a baptism of repentance for the forgiveness of sins. The whole Judean countryside and all the people of Jerusalem went out to him. Confessing their sins, they were baptized by him in the Jordan River. John wore clothing made of camel's hair, with a leather belt around his waist, and he ate locusts and wild honey. And this was his message: "After me comes the one more powerful than I, the straps of whose sandals I am not worthy to stoop down and untie. I baptize you with water, but he will baptize you with the Holy Spirit."

— Mark 1:1–8

Dear Mark the Scrooge,

Your Gospel seems to introduce us to the first "scrooge like" character in the New Testament, and it's you. Mark, why did you skip the Christmas story? Come on! Your friend Matthew hung his holiday lights before anyone else on the block, and your friend Luke loved Christmas so much that he left milk and cookies out for Santa. All three of you borrowed from one another to tell Jesus's story, but you chose to be the scrooge. There is always one scrooge in the group.

    I know you were in a hurry, but you shouldn't have lopped off Christmas. Your Gospel is the shortest of them all. It's full of movement. You weren't interested in feelings or any unnecessary words. You made your point, got right to the action, and moved on. When I try to read your gospel in one sitting, I break out into a sweat. I feel like I'm running and reading at the same time. I suppose if I reign in your Gospel and slow it down a bit, I might find a few hints of Christmas.

    So, I want to give your Gospel a chance this Christmas season. You skipped the Christmas details we have come to love in the Gospels to the left and to the right of yours, speaking of Matthew and Luke. But again, if we slow down and read carefully, we might catch a glimpse of holiday spirit.

    You jumped right into it. You didn't see the birth and nativity set details as important. You skipped right to Jesus the adult. I mean your opening line reads, "The beginning of the good news about Jesus the Messiah." You had no time for Jesus, Immanuel, you moved right ahead to Jesus, Messiah. But we do have language that at least points to the coming of the Christ. You did use words like, "send," "messenger," "make," "calling," "prepare," and "way." These are all Christmas words. These words are filled with anticipation and excitement. They point to something new and different. Maybe nodding to the Christmas story, just in your own way. You pointed to another type of birth. Another type of coming. A birth that points to the coming of Jesus's ministry, rather than Jesus's infancy. I guess this is the Christmas story too. The coming of the Christ is not just the baby birth and all its familiar details. Sure, those things make for a fun Christmas, but there is so much more.

We also need to understand what happened because He was born. You almost insinuated, "Okay, He was born—big deal. But now what?" And you were excited about the "now what." It's as if you were saying, "Because of the quaint Christmas details that my friends Matthew and Luke gave you, I can skip right to the good stuff." His real birth will actually be His birth into Messiahhood. Yes, baby Jesus was cute. Yes, teenage Jesus in the temple was heart-warming. But you moved us right to the good stuff: Jesus as Messiah. Jesus as minister. Jesus as healer. Jesus as the person who would move quickly toward the cross and change the world.

Perhaps you were the real holiday lover here because you understood the real meaning of Christmas. Sort of like the person who gets all excited about the gifts, the tree, the food, and the drinks, versus the person who celebrates for the right reason—the recognition of the reality of Jesus Messiah. Thanks, Mark. Thanks for playing the role of scrooge. But maybe you're the one who truly got it. And the only one who gives it too. You give us the real meaning of Christmas. You are all in for Jesus. And that is how it should be.

Matthew hung his lights early, Luke set out the milk and cookies, but you gave us Jesus. And in giving us Jesus, you gave us Christmas. You're no scrooge, Mark. You just understood the Christmas story in a way the rest of us didn't. Thanks for the reminder, and thanks for putting Jesus back into Christmas.

DAY 23

DEAR MATTHEW

"At that time the kingdom of heaven will be like ten virgins who took their lamps and went out to meet the bridegroom. Five of them were foolish and five were wise. The foolish ones took their lamps but did not take any oil with them. The wise ones, however, took oil in jars along with their lamps. The bridegroom was a long time in coming, and they all became drowsy and fell asleep.

"At midnight the cry rang out: 'Here's the bridegroom! Come out to meet him!'

"Then all the virgins woke up and trimmed their lamps. The foolish ones said to the wise, 'Give us some of your oil; our lamps are going out.'

"'No,' they replied, 'there may not be enough for both us and you. Instead, go to those who sell oil and buy some for yourselves.'

"But while they were on their way to buy the oil, the bridegroom arrived. The virgins who were ready went in with him to the wedding banquet. And the door was shut.

"Later the others also came. 'Lord, Lord,' they said, 'open the door for us!'

"But he replied, 'Truly I tell you, I don't know you.'

> "Therefore keep watch, because you do not know the day or the hour."
>
> — Matthew 25:1-13

Dear Matthew,

I'm familiar with your parable of the ten virgins simply because I've attended both church and Bible class all my life. I suppose all the parables, miracles, and classic Old Testament stories are stuck in my brain, much like the scent of my laundry detergent sticks to my clothes. But that doesn't mean I can tell you everything there is to know about the detergent.

The story of the ten virgins certainly does not make my top ten list of all-time favorite parables, Matthew. When I first read it, it also didn't give me warm fuzzies about Christmas. But again, like a good church boy, I know the basic details of your story. Without even reviewing the text, I remember that ten virgins decided to attend a wedding. Maybe they were part of the official wedding party, I forget. I remember that five virgins took torches that had no oil, and five virgins had torches and back up oil to go along with them. Of course, today this makes no sense because we have electricity, and we don't tend to have weddings that last for several hours with the crescendo sometimes not happening until the wee hours of the morning. I'm told orthodox weddings in the Mediterranean world still follow this tradition. But this story doesn't quite resonate with a westerner.

So, back to the meaning of your parable. Five were prepared and five weren't. The five who weren't prepared didn't bring enough fuel. So, they asked their prepared friends to share, to which request the others said no, and to go and buy their own oil. Then, the bridegroom came, and the door was slammed in their faces. Not only did the wedding party slam the door on them, but apparently the kingdom of God did as well.

I don't like this parable you tell, Matthew. I mean Jesus spoke plainly a few dozen pages earlier in your own Gospel about walking two miles instead of one and giving up your cloak to someone in need. So, this parable seems odd, cold, and maybe even misplaced.

I realize that you are the author and were also an eye witness, but if I were to give my thoughts on this parable centuries later as an armchair Bible scholar, I might say that the coming of the Lord spoken about here is the coming of the Christ in terms of his lordship, not the return of Christ in the last days. In other words, this is not a condemnation to hell, but a reminder that Christ has come, and you can't borrow someone else's faith. Instead, you ought to see Christ and His reign right here and now, for yourself.

Or perhaps, I would comment that the very next parable involves foolish decisions on the parts of men. Both men and women—all humanity—need to peel back the scales from their eyes and see the coming of the Christ. Or perhaps this story would have made perfect sense to a Jew, which I realize was your primary audience.

Maybe it's not very humble of me to weigh in with my opinion, since you are the author of the story. But I choose to take a more mystical and liberal interpretation of what you wrote, Matthew. One that is not so dualistic in thought, not so black and white, not so either/or, but rather one that is both/and, that opens possibilities that would rekindle my love for this section of the Bible, so I'd no longer want to avoid it.

Maybe you just miss it.

After all, you were recording these details much later than when they were told. There were no dictation devices, no smart phones with handy voice recording applications. Did you really hear it this way, word for word? Because I'm trying to understand this story considering the other red letters, Red letters that I like better. Red letters that are dark and unmistakably red. Matthew, are you sure this is supposed to be red letter stuff?

You speak of these five virgins who had the door slammed in their faces and left in darkness. But in a few days, your Messiah would struggle too. In fact, the door would be slammed on Him, and He would be in darkness. The Messiah, while hanging in darkness, even had a thing or two to say to His father regarding this.

Maybe Jesus should have been more prepared. He knew the time was coming. He had time to muster up maximum willpower. Maybe He just wasn't quite prepared for the big moment. And while I'm on a roll: Do you recall the story of the slamming of the door at the motel office the night Jesus was born on the first ever Christmas Eve? Think about how that made His parents feel.

Or maybe both things are true. Maybe the point of this is to keep us on our toes. Both perspectives are true. Should we be ready? Yes, you bet. Is this serious stuff? No doubt. Should we be disciplined and morally upright as we anticipate the last days? Of course. At the same time, Matthew, you might be a little off. This must be heard in context with the very heart and nature of God, and the last words His Son spoke. Matthew, thanks for the reminder that I need to be prepared—that's more than fair.

But now let me remind you of something, Matthew. Because of Advent, I feel I can boldly claim that Jesus came for the sick. Jesus came for the ones who kept forgetting. Jesus came for the ones who didn't have the resources for the extra fuel in the first place. Thanks for the reminder to live in this incredible tension, Matthew. God knows I need more discipline in my life. But the words that are the reddest in my heart and soul tell me that at the end of the day, and at the last hour, all I can and will do is throw myself at the mercy seat of my Lord and beg Him to fill me with His limitless resources of goodness and love. Matthew, maybe the fact that Jesus endured the slamming of the door on the first Christmas Eve means that we will never have to.

DAY 24

DEAR STRUGGLER

Then Herod called the Magi secretly and found out from them the exact time the star had appeared. He sent them to Bethlehem and said, "Go and search carefully for the child. As soon as you find him, report to me, so that I too may go and worship him." After they had heard the king, they went on their way, and the star they had seen when it rose went ahead of them until it stopped over the place where the child was. When they saw the star, they were overjoyed. On coming to the house, they saw the child with his mother Mary, and they bowed down and worshiped him. Then they opened their treasures and presented him with gifts of gold, frankincense and myrrh. And having been warned in a dream not to go back to Herod, they returned to their country by another route. When they had gone, an angel of the Lord appeared to Joseph in a dream. "Get up," he said, "take the child and his mother and escape to Egypt. Stay there until I tell you, for Herod is going to search for the child to kill him." So he got up, took the child and his mother during the night and left for Egypt, where he stayed until the death of Herod. And so was fulfilled what the Lord had said through the prophet: "Out of Egypt I called my son." When Herod realized that he had been outwitted by the Magi, he was furious, and he gave orders to kill all the boys in Bethlehem and its vicinity who were two years old and under, in accordance with the time he had learned from the Magi.

— Matthew 2:7–16

Dear Struggler,

Matthew gives it to us straight. When it comes to the Christmas narrative, Matthew told the entire story, not just the part that creates perfect nativity sets, lights, and gifts. He assumed his readers could handle it, so he was honest. Luke was the physician, but Matthew took on the role of the stoic and honest doctor, giving the family the up front and honest news after surgery. No sugar coating. No warm fuzzies. Just tell me. And Matthew did.

If you only want singing angels, worshiping shepherds, and a perfect baby in a manger, no need for you to read on. But if you are like me and want the entire story, the good with the bad, the authentic version versus the children's book version, then proceed—this might be the Advent story you've been craving but have never heard. Part of the Christmas story entails untold pain and suffering that I never heard anyone talk about when I was growing up. Again, if we want it straight, Matthew is the right Gospel to turn to.

My sister is a therapist, and she tells me therapists are busier around the holiday season than any other time of the year because there are two sides to Christmas: there is the Charlie Brown and Hallmark movie side, and then there is the side that brings extra hurt. If you've experienced pain, then that pain is typically only increased with the arrival of Christmas. If your marriage is out of tune, if you've lost a job, if your kids are struggling, then those things seem darker and more daunting at Christmas. But you've come to the right place; you've come to get the Christmas story from Matthew.

Matthew is the only Gospel writer who tells us of King Herod and his plans to ruin Christmas. Herod heard a baby king would be born in Bethlehem, so he sent out his messengers, the wisemen (yes, the same wisemen who end up in the Nativity set) to find the baby King and report back to him. Herod wanted to kill baby Jesus, but he told the wisemen a different story. Well, the wisemen became convinced that the baby King really was the Messiah. They took an alternate route home to avoid Herod. At the same time, Joseph received a warning about Herod in a dream, so he fled to Egypt with his little family to escape the wrath of the madman.

When King Herod discovered that he'd been hoodwinked by the faithful wisemen, he retaliated with quite the decree. He sent out his army, and he ordered them to kill every baby boy throughout the land that was two years old or younger. Yes, you read that correctly. Because of Jesus's birth, thousands of baby boys were murdered. This reality is part of the Christmas story: innocent baby boys were slaughtered while their moms and dads wept. Yep, "Joy to the world, the Lord has come," and then there were parents throughout the region burying their baby boys. That doesn't make such a catchy Christmas tune, does it?

My goal is not to ruin your Christmas or your faith with this honest and graphic retelling. My goal is to give you the gospel. You see, besides this dark story, there is one more thing that's unique to the Gospel of Matthew. He's the only Gospel writer who tells us Jesus's name at birth. And that's Immanuel, which means "God with us." Did you hear that? He is the God who is with us. Matthew knew life happens. Matthew knew that some Christmases would be dark. Because of that, he gave us the all-important reminder that this God we now have, this baby Messiah and Savior of the world, has a name. And that name means "He is with us." He is with us when there's a crazy killer on the loose. He is with us while we take a long, hard journey. He is with us in loneliness. He is with us in sickness. He is with us when Christmas is bright and filled with joy, and He is with us when Christmas is dark. He is with us.

Matthew tells us the authentic and real version. And you know what? I'm glad he does. Because that's exactly how life happens. It ebbs and flows. It brings great joy and great lament. It brings both great happiness and great pain. There is no getting around that. So, whether this is a Hallmark Christmas or one full of therapy appointments, we can rest assured on one promise: God's name is Immanuel and that means He joins us right where we are. Always.

DAY 25

DEAR GOD

So all the elders of Israel gathered together and came to Samuel at Ramah. They said to him, "You are old, and your sons do not follow your ways; now appoint a king to lead us, such as all the other nations have."

But when they said, "Give us a king to lead us," this displeased Samuel; so he prayed to the Lord.

And the Lord told him: "Listen to all that the people are saying to you; it is not you they have rejected, but they have rejected me as their king. As they have done from the day I brought them up out of Egypt until this day, forsaking me and serving other gods, so they are doing to you. Now listen to them; but warn them solemnly and let them know what the king who will reign over them will claim as his rights."

— 1 Samuel 8:4–9

Dear God,

Your people have always wanted a king. A mighty, majestic, and powerful king. But You, in Your infinite wisdom, knew better.

The people begged You, and You said no. They pleaded with You, and You warned them. But finally, like a loving Father who sometimes just throws his arms up, You gave in to their whining and constant nagging. I wonder if You thought to Yourself that it might work. Or if You were just sick of their complaining and wanted to shut them up. Good dads do that sometimes. Either way, You granted their request. I love the fact that You allow Your children to make their own decisions. I love the fact that every so often, You let us talk You into something. It has always made You seem more accessible to me, more real to me, more human to me.

Well, we now know their request for a king didn't turn out so well. Most of the kings were corrupt. Your people looked to them for security. They asked their kings to oppress others for their safety and peace. All these things made You sad, I'm sure. I think You always preferred them follow You as King, but You knew their desire to have someone in the flesh.

We've always preferred things that we can see, touch, talk to, and try to manipulate. And even though it seems we'd be better off with just You; that probably won't ever work because we can't see You, we can't seem to hear Your audible voice. Perhaps someday You will explain to us why a healthy distance from You seems to be the best thing. But in the meantime, we need a physical king.

Hundreds of years passed, with one failure of a king after another—and then You gave us a real King, One who would never be corrupt or fail. In Your own Son, You gave us the perfect, And just as your people began to puff our their chests, just as they began to brag to the rival country next door, just as they began to sit back and daydream about their enemies being struck down, they found out the King you gave came as a baby. A helpless baby, born of a virgin with not one drop of royalty in her blood, and Son to a blue-collar carpenter with blisters on his hands; one who was announced to the world by lowly shepherds and born in an animal stable.

Maybe your people thought it was a joke, but we know it wasn't; it's real. And it's called Christmas. It's Your fatherly answer to Your people's cries and pleas. A little baby born in a backwater town—that's our

King. For years, we've been fighting it. We still want power. We still want control. We still want You to kill our enemies. But every year, for a few weeks around Christmas, our clarity returns. We remember. Our vision comes into focus. Our hearts soften. We complain a little less and love a little more. You found a way to give us Yourself at Christmas. This Advent season—Christmastime—provides the grace which covers the rest of the calendar year. Thank you, God. Thank You for finding a path to be our King—our baby King. Thank You for Christmas.

EPILOGUE

DEAR SANTA

Dear Santa,

I hope you're safely back at the North Pole and prepping for a long, peaceful slumber. The work you do is important work, but I believe it takes a lot out of you. The kids stayed up again this year looking for you, but like every year, they didn't see you. They saw signs of you, of course, but they always hope to get a glimpse of you—the real you.

We left cookies out for you, snuffed the flames out in our fireplace, and monitored your progress on our Santa Tracker app. That's the best we could do. I've been talking about you for decades. Hoping in you. Defending you. Holding fascination for you. Buying the movies you star in. Looking forward to your visit each year.

But I've never seen you, never actually laid eyes on you. I've seen people mimic and imitate you, but they seem to always fall short. I want you to know, however, that I keep believing. Against all odds, I keep believing. Some years I believe with passion. Other years, it's a struggle, but I usually find an ounce of belief. I believe in you for one reason. And that's because I think you are worth believing in.

I mean what's not to like about you and what you stand for? Based on my experience: You're kind, fair, gentle, intuitive, and full of generosity and hospitality. I mean radical generosity. You lavishly give of yourself to the entire world. Those are things I want to believe in.

And I want you to know the stakes are high here, Santa. Because I'm telling my kids you're real. I'm backing you up, even though every year they wait up faithfully to see you, yet don't. I want them to hold on to that hope. It seems like next to death and taxes, the one thing we can count on in this life is trauma. Trauma, and some pain along the way, seem to be part of what it means to be human. So, a strong dose of hope is something worth holding on to.

You see, Santa, there is someone else I am trying to convince my children is real, and I have a hunch they will never see this person, either. And that is God. Some people refer to Him in different ways. God, Jesus, Spirit, Loving Creator—I think you get the point. I want them to hold on to the realness of an all-loving being who is loving them and reconciling the world as they move through it. Because that also seems worth believing in. I've weighed the alternatives. I understand the differing philosophical positions. Perhaps the only true place to land is agnosticism, but I like the idea of hope. Hope makes us a little lighter. Hope causes us to smile a bit more. Hope creates reason to keep going, when otherwise it doesn't make sense. Hope seems to produce the kind of life that ends up being well-lived.

Every time I see generosity, each time I witness hospitality, any time I see someone creating a little magic in someone else's life, I think of you, Santa, and what you stand for. And it's good. It's worth believing in. So, because of that, we will once again leave cookies out. We will stamp out the flames. We will stay up late into the evening until our eyelids are heavy. We will look, we will listen, we will wait, and we will hope.

FINAL LETTER OF ENCOURAGEMENT FROM THE AUTHOR

When I think of beginnings and starting points, I think of a spark Just a spark can lead to a roaring fire. A spark of encouragement can lead to a profound idea or discovery. Sparks oftentimes index the beginning of something. However, sparks can also come at other times and in other ways.

One of the unexpected blessings of the Covid-19 pandemic, and the "shelter in place" orders that came with it, was the opportunity it provided to connect with one of my neighbors in a deeper, more profound way. The pandemic created a context where casual hellos were traded for prolonged conversations between my neighbor and I because neither of us had anywhere to go.

So, we developed a routine of nightly gathering and sparking conversation around a firepit on the patio. Because evenings outside in Michigan call for a fire. Typically, in the early stages of the fire, while the kindling was producing sparks, our families would come outside and exchange niceties. The kids would run around for a moment; therefore, small talk was in order. However, when the kids went inside and the evening became still, and the fire calmed to nothing but smoldering coals with the occasional spark, God would do His best work.

The early sparks that would get the fire roaring were undoubtedly important. However, rich and authentic conversation never took place over those initial sparks. Rather, it was always during the sparks at the very end, as the fire was waning, and the kids retreated inside. When it was just the two of us, my neighbor and I, left in the light of the barely burning embers, God seemed to show up.

This was when tough questions were asked. This was when we answered questions with honesty. This was when my neighbor, who's now well past middle age, would ask questions about the existence of God and the legitimacy of the Bible. God not only works within the early stages of belief, in the sparks that lead to a roaring fire of faith; God also works later in life, in the embers, in the smoldering wood has been burning a long time.

My neighbor had rejected the idea of faith in the Son of God and the Bible. For 56 years, in fact, there was no raging fire. But now, around a friendly fire, late at night, he's asking; he's inquiring; he's open. And the smoldering coals of his heart are beginning to catch the wind, momentum, strength, and grow. I'm looking forward to watching God work with those catching sparks.

Sometimes God does his best work well into the evening, and at the last moment. God can work with the sparks that ignite the fire early on, and He can work with the sparks as the fire is going out. He never gives up. He has no preference. He's ready. He can work at any moment and with any level of faith. He's always ready.

It is easy to have a spark when we gaze into the eyes of baby Jesus. But time settles in, and that spark can cool off. My prayer is that something was read in this book that brought your spark back. But, in a few days, it will be time again to take down the tree and pack up the decorations. The colder months will come and there will be no twinkling lights to look at, which bring cheer. But God is near. God is present. He can do great work with the smallest flicker of faith, even when the world is dark and cold. Hang on. Keep the faith. Fan that flame within. And before you know it, next year's Advent season will be upon us…

You've honored me by reading these letters.

– Klint Pleasant

DR. KLINT PLEASANT is the Senior Vice President, Special Assistant to the President, and Men's Head Basketball Coach at Rochester University. Under his leadership and coaching, he has led his teams to two National Championships, and multiple top 25 NAIA National Rankings and Tournament appearances, including wins over NCAA I and II teams. He's won Coach of the Year honors in 2015, 2016 and 2021, and his teams have average over 21 wins per year. Prior to coaching at Rochester University, Pleasant was Head Coach for Men's Basketball at Abilene Christian University, and Assistant Coach for Men's Basketball at Kent State University, The University of Tennessee at Martin, and Wayne State University. While at Kent State, he helped lead the team to an Elite Eight appearance in the 2001 NCAA I National Basketball Tournament. Pleasant earned his Doctoral degree in educational leadership and administration from Lipscomb University in 2019. He is an avid Keynote speaker on topics of leadership, team building, creating healthy culture, overcoming adversity, and managing change. He also is a sought-after presenter at retreats and business consulting events. He and his wife have negotiated trauma and it has shaped his faith and ability to help lead others. His wife's name is Rachel, and they has two precious daughters, Abbey and Julia. And a dog named Captain (named after a Pearl Jam song, who he's been known to follow around the country). As a leader and administrator, Pleasant still values listening, learning, authenticity, and having meaningful conversations to always seek better understanding.

Made in the USA
Las Vegas, NV
05 December 2021